What Martial Arts Taught Me About The Gospel Of Jesus Christ

Spiritual Lessons From The Dojo

Glyn Norman

Copyright © 2012 Glyn Norman

All rights reserved.

ISBN: 1499793499
ISBN-13: 978-1499793499

DEDICATION

With thanks to Rich Scott, and Master James White, my martial arts instructors – with gratitude for all they taught me.

To Landon, my wonderful son, who is still a higher belt than me.

And with thanks to my Lord and Savior Jesus Christ, who enables me to stand firm.

GLYN NORMAN

CONTENTS

1	Introduction	1
2	Know When To Tap Out	3
3	The Importance of Discipline	11
4	Be Aware - Evil Is Out There	31
5	With Great Power Comes Great Responsibility	37
6	The Power in Perseverance	41

1. INTRODUCTION

I started martial arts when I was 20 years old. I had become a Christian a few months earlier, and one day went to the Carnival in Herne Bay, where the Jiu-Jitsu club was giving a demonstration. I was very impressed by the control they had over their bodies, and the ease with which they seemed to deal with potential attacks. After chatting to a few of them and making some inquiries, I decided to join them, and so started my experience in martial arts.

Perhaps because both Christianity and martial arts were so new to me, I quickly saw parallels between the two "pursuits" and this book is an attempt to explain how some of the elements of martial arts relate very neatly to the practices of Christianity.

At the outset it is important to note that the style of martial arts I was involved with had no connection to Eastern Mysticism, as some of them do. There was no meditation, chanting, humming "Om" or any other practices more commonly associated with Eastern Mysticism. My instructor was a very down-to-earth police sergeant, and his comments were not generally along spiritual lines. More common would be something like, "Well lads, last Saturday night, this youth came at me with a bottle, so I blocked it, locked his arm behind his back and marched him to my squad car. Let me show you the move I used." This would then be followed by a practical demonstration, though we used plastic bottles to avoid the potential injuries of novices. It was always entertaining and informative to hear first-hand how these techniques we were learning had actually worked in a real-life street situation.

I was a part of this Jiu-Jitsu club until I moved away to London and went to seminary where I gained my degree in Theology. After college, I moved to Germany, then California, then Florida, where I finally picked up martial arts again, though in a different discipline: Tae Kwon Do. In those intervening years I had occasion to use my martial arts skills twice in real life, once to protect myself, and once to rescue a girl who was being manhandled by a somewhat brutal guy. Well, he was brutal up to the point when I put him in a painful wrist-lock, but you'll read more about that one later.

My hope is that out of this small book you will gain some insights which will enable you to live out your Christianity with more of a warrior spirit, with determination, and with utter dedication to the one who died for you. If you are not a Christian, I hope the perspective of a fellow martial-artist will make sense to you and hopefully make clearer the gospel of Jesus Christ.

2. KNOW WHEN TO TAP OUT

I remember my first Jiu-Jitsu practice very well, probably because it is associated in my mind with serious pain, both during the practice and afterward. The practice started with about one hour of physical conditioning training. I had thought I was in fairly good shape (I played in a table-tennis league, which in England is a real sport) but this one hour revealed to me the reality of the matter. I was a lot less fit than I had imagined. There were countless exercises involving push-ups, sit-ups, jumping jacks, running... and on and on it went. For the first ten minutes I kept up well enough, but then I started to fade and lose my breath. The remainder of that first hour was a struggle, to say the least.

In the second hour, we practiced techniques, for example, how to respond to a punch, someone trying to strangle you from in front or behind, how to escape from a headlock and so on. The general sequence was that your first response would be to strike the attacker in some way. For example, if they were strangling you from the front, you would kick at their knee. This would have the effect of loosening their grip, which would then free you to do your next maneuver. The kick, or first strike was known as "the weakener" and we would usually practice it with just a light touch, since if you really get properly kicked in the knee, that's going to be the end of the practice for you, and probably for quite a few weeks. So, as their hands wrapped around your throat, you would kick out and just brush their knee with your foot. The person grabbing you would loosen their hands a little, to simulate the actual loosening that would occur with a real kick, and then you would continue, usually with a follow-up strike, or some sort of "lock" which meant twisting one of their limbs into such a painful position that they would surrender.

This was all excellent fun, and I learned so much even in that first evening. There was one key element that they forgot to teach me though - how to 'tap out.' For those unfamiliar with martial arts, tapping out refers to a type of signal you give when the other person has you in that painful position, and you wish to indicate surrender. In our club, it meant tapping twice on the mat or on their body so they would know not to increase the pressure any more. As I was on the floor, in some considerable pain from the wrist-lock someone had placed on me, they kept increasing the pressure until I finally cried out. They looked at me and asked, "Why didn't you tap out?" When I told them I didn't know what it was, they laughed and then explained it to me. This one explanation saved me a lot of pain in the ensuing years!

There's a lesson for life there too. How many of us fail to tap out, either because we don't know it is an option, or we are simply too proud to admit the pain we are in? This pain need not be physical. It can be spiritual, psychological, emotional or any other type of pain. The point is, we can each come to a point in our lives where we are at the end of ourselves. We come to a point where we really need outside help, because our own resources are depleted or inadequate for the challenges we face.

To admit that we need help can be humbling and so many of us shy away from it. Both cultures with which I am familiar have a strong tradition of independence, rather than inter-dependence. Growing up as a young boy in England, I was regaled through comics and other media, with stories of our triumph over the evil of Nazi Germany in the Second World War. In many of these stories, it was the plucky Brits who, like an earwig cornered, refused to give up despite the odds, and fought on, eventually winning the day. It was only later in life that I realized how incredibly dependent victory was. Without the assistance of the other allies, particularly the USA and Russia, we would not have prevailed.

In the United States, the pioneer spirit has fueled movies and literature ever since the colonists started moving West. This was a time when the hardy survived, through their own ingenuity and sheer grit. Freedom and independence are still powerful currents in American society, and even depending in part on the government for assistance smacks of socialism to many, and is looked down upon.

The fact is that most of us, especially men, are taught a lesson early in life, that we can only depend on ourselves. Our individual ability and prowess is paramount. Only the weak need help. Only the very weak admit that they need help.

For me, the lesson that I need to admit it when I am powerless and need relief came most painfully in that martial arts lesson. But it had also come a few months earlier, as I had to make a similar admission, but this time, in the spiritual realm.

I was on the outside, a reasonably confident 20 year old, working in real estate, interested in girls, cars and making money (which I assumed would help with the girls and cars.) Inside though, there was a different story going on. There was a spiritual gulf within me. I knew something was missing; I just didn't know what it was.

I had been brought up in the Catholic Church, and had gone through the rites of passage such as First Communion, and Confirmation. I learned to say the right things, and when to stand up, when to kneel, and was even an altar boy at one point. My primary (elementary) school was Catholic and we were taught in some classes by nuns. On Wednesday afternoon, as part of the school day, we were taken to church for "Benediction," a service which included prayers in Latin and incense (which I unwisely told the headmaster I didn't like). I was steeped in Catholic practice, but honestly, for me the ritual obscured the spiritual reality behind it. For many, it can be that this ritual assists them in sensing a connection to God, but for me it did not. When I left primary school at age 11, I had nothing more to do with religion or church. I did study Religion in Secondary (High) School, but it was merely an academic pursuit.

When I was 20, I joined a table-tennis club, and soon became friends with a player named John. As we talked, he was quite open about the fact that he was a Christian, and to my surprise, did not seem embarrassed by this fact. What was more confusing to me was that he seemed quite normal! I don't know where my mental image of a Christian had come from, but somehow they seemed to be weak and wimpy characters, soft-spoken, apologetic, pasty-white and somewhat otherworldly. John was not like that at all. He embraced life with a sense of wonderment and great humor, and I was drawn to him. He spoke about his relationship with Jesus as though he were a friend.

Often, after our table-tennis practices, we would go back to his mother's house and discuss the questions I had about Christianity. I guess they were much the same as most people have:

- why does Christianity claim to be the only way to God? What about other religions? (I had studied Buddhism at school, and was impressed with it as a philosophy)
- if there is a good God, why is there so much suffering in the world? If he is good, and if he is all-powerful, why doesn't he do something about it?
- isn't the Bible full of contradictions, and out of date? How can you trust it and think it is relevant?

With great patience, and a good deal of intelligence John attempted to answer my questions. He was a lawyer, and knew how to structure a logical argument, and for the first time, Christianity was presented to me as a rational step. There were some questions he could not answer and I appreciated his honesty in that. When he told me there were some things I would have to accept by faith, he was not advocating that I check my brain at the door. He was pointing out that there are some things about an infinite God which, since we are finite human beings, might be beyond our comprehension. I could accept that. I wasn't arrogant enough to think that if there was a God, he would be within the power of my brain to fully understand.

After we had been friends for a few months, John invited me to attend a church service with him, at his local church - Tankerton Evangelical. At first I was hesitant but then finally agreed, thinking to myself that I could endure a 1.5 hour service, however bad it was. If I could sit through Catholic services in Latin where I didn't understand a thing, I would be able to manage this.

Unknown to John, before I attended that first time, I made a deal with God, along the following lines: "God, if you exist, which I don't know for sure, then I'll make a deal with you. You have one month to convince me that you are real, that you know me and that you love me. If I don't sense that after going to church with John four times, then I'm done with you." I felt pretty confident that I had set the bar high enough that God would not come through, and I could with a clear conscience tell John that I had tried it, and that it didn't work for me.

The first Sunday I attended, I walked into church worried. I wasn't just worried about the unfamiliarity of the church service. I was worried about financial issues. I had a job in real estate that was mostly commission-based, and it was not going well. The most pressing issue on my mind as I sat down for that first service was worry about finances. After the songs, the preacher, Rev. John Bishop came up to the pulpit and said he was going to preach about our attitude toward material things and money. This caught my attention, as I was certainly in the right frame of mind to hear something encouraging about that issue. The passage he spoke on was from the Sermon on the Mount, where Jesus is preaching. Here are the nine verses that rocked my world:

> 25 "Therefore I tell you, do not be anxious about your life, what you will eat or what you will drink, nor about your body, what you will put on. Is not life more than food, and the body more than clothing? 26 Look at the birds of the air: they neither sow nor reap nor gather into barns, and yet your heavenly Father feeds them. Are you not of more value than they? 27 And which of you by being anxious can add a single hour to his span of life? 28 And why are you anxious about clothing? Consider the lilies of the field, how they grow: they neither toil nor spin, 29 yet I tell you, even Solomon in all his glory was not arrayed like one of these. 30 But if God so clothes the grass of the field, which today is alive and tomorrow is thrown into the oven, will he not much more clothe you, O you of little faith? 31 Therefore do not be anxious, saying, 'What shall we eat?' or 'What shall we drink?' or 'What shall we wear?' 32 For the Gentiles seek after all these things, and your heavenly Father knows that you need them all. 33 But seek first the kingdom of God and his

righteousness, and all these things will be added to you.

34 "Therefore do not be anxious about tomorrow, for tomorrow will be anxious for itself. Sufficient for the day is its own trouble. (Matthew 6:25-34)

For the first time in a long time, I started to consider the possibility that maybe there was something more to life than money (or specifically, my lack of it). It was as though my head, which was weighed down in anxiety, was caused to look up and consider that there was perhaps something more out there. I was also impressed that the preacher had "luckily" hit on the very issue that was occupying my mind that morning. I had to grudgingly admit to John that what was preached that day was actually relevant to me.

The next week, I entered with a little trepidation wondering if the preacher was going to get lucky again with his choice of topic. The issue that was most on my mind that week was my relationship with my girlfriend, which was going through a rocky patch. In fact, I wasn't sure we would be a couple for very much longer. Again, after the songs, Rev. Bishop got up, and said: "Today, I'm going to talk about God's guide to relationships." Gulp. Not again. How did he know? I whispered quickly to John, asking him if he had told the preacher what I was dealing with, but he assured me he had said nothing, and as I thought about it, I didn't even remember mentioning my relationship troubles to John, so that couldn't be it. Through that sermon, I started understanding that God's blueprint for relationships was very different from mine: living selflessly rather than selfishly; considering others needs instead of just my own... This was starting to hit a bit close to the bone.

I went back the third week, and again, the sermon was precisely on the issue that was troubling me. The fourth week it happened again, and I couldn't take it anymore. It could not have been more clear to me that God had won my wager. Through every one of those sermons I had heard, he had shown that he knew my situation, cared about me, and wanted to show me a different path.

This was my crisis point. This was where I had to decide to tap out, to admit to God that I could not run my life on my own; that doing it my way was not working out, and that I needed him. As I made that decision, as I called out to God to rescue me, to lift me out of my troubles, to relieve my guilt and shame, a physical sensation washed over me. It was as though my heart was burning within me. I later found a Bible verse which described what I had felt:

> And I will give you a new heart, and a new spirit I will put within you. And I will remove the heart of stone from your flesh and give you a heart of flesh. (Ezekiel 36:26).

That was exactly how it felt, as though my stony heart had been made soft. As the service concluded, I told John that I had decided that I wanted to follow Jesus. He offered to introduce me to the preacher, and together we prayed a prayer where I gave my heart to Jesus and told him that I wanted to live his way rather than my way.

Twenty-seven years later, I am a pastor in a church in Florida, having studied theology in London, served as a missionary in Berlin, and as a pastor in California. I am still in touch with John, and remind him that he seriously messed up my life by inviting me to church!

The interesting part for me is that I still need to remember to tap out. I still drift into believing that I can lead this life with my own strength and wisdom. I think that I have what it takes, and God has to remind me that I need him. He reminds me that I was not designed to be independent, but to be in relationship with him. When I live that way, it goes better. When I tap out, when I run to pray, when I acknowledge my own weakness, then He is made strong in me.

I don't know where you are at. Perhaps you would not call yourself a Christian, but you are feeling the pressure. Maybe some crisis has come upon you or maybe just the regular pressures of life (bills, parenting, job stress) are weighing you down to the point of feeling overwhelmed. The good news of the gospel is that you don't need to walk this path alone. This is Jesus' invitation, in the Gospel of Matthew:

28 Come to me, all who labor and are heavy laden, and I will give you rest. 29 Take my yoke upon you, and learn from me, for I am gentle and lowly in heart, and you will find rest for your souls. 30 For my yoke is easy, and my burden is light." (Matthew 11:28-30)

I have heard the oft-repeated criticism that Christianity is a crutch for the weak. To which my answer is, if you have a broken leg, or even a twisted ankle, a crutch is a good thing, and there's no embarrassment in having one. For each of us, we experience a degree of brokenness. We are people who are wounded and broken. We are sinners, and we are sinned against. Life does something to us, and there is no shame in getting to the point of admitting that we need help, that we cannot walk this path alone. The truth is, we were never designed to. Life was intended to be a partnership between the created and the Creator, in harmony together.

It is my experience that only the very proud or foolish will state that they never need any help. If ever I hear this, I know that I could come back in 10 years and probably hear a different answer. Life has a way of teaching us that our resources are finite, and that our individual strength is not enough.

For me, in that dojo, all those years ago, there was no embarrassment about tapping out. When I did, the person released the grip, and offered a hand to help me up. Will you be honest enough, humble enough to take the hand of Jesus that is reached out to you?

3. THE IMPORTANCE OF DISCIPLINE

If you are ever in a threatening situation, it is likely that your body will experience a surge of adrenaline. Theoretically, the function of adrenaline is to make you faster, stronger, and less receptive to pain. In reality, this sudden surge can cause your hands to shake, and for you to feel quite weak. My martial arts instructor explained that it was common to feel about 20-30% less strong in an actual situation of confrontation. This was his rationale behind all of the conditioning training that we used to do. His theory was that if we became 20-30% stronger than we had initially been, the feeling of weakness would be offset by our superior physical conditioning.

After the first practice, I was out of breath, extremely thirsty and felt exhausted and slightly nauseous. I thought this was as bad as it gets, but I was wrong. That first practice was on a Monday night, and on Tuesday morning I could hardly get out of bed. My muscles were stiff as a board, and it took a massive, painful effort even to get to the bathroom. I somehow struggled through that day, though walking like a zombie, and woke up the next morning, with only a slight improvement. I reasoned that the only way to get this dealt with was to go the martial arts club that night, exercise again, and hope that the kinks would be worked out. After a few painful minutes, that was what happened. I don't know if I just loosened up, or if pain-relieving chemicals flooded my body, but somehow after that practice it became a whole lot easier.

Through the first hour of conditioning training I learned discipline of action. From the second hour of techniques training, I learned discipline of reaction. The first hour was where we conditioned our bodies to cope with the demands, the strength and reflexes required in the second hour. Of course, both hours were preparation for real life where, if ever you needed to, you would have the ability to defend yourself, or intervene to protect someone else.

The Christian life involves disciplines of action and reaction too. It is often when you have engaged in the disciplines of action, that the disciplines of reaction become a whole lot easier. The lessons learned, often in the quietness of your own study or prayer time, are the ones that inform and enable you to respond correctly when confronted with real life situations.

Steven Covey, in his excellent book, The 7 Habits of Highly Effective People, says that we should take advantage of the short time that exists between stimulus and response. If we simply act out of our natural instinct, it will be a reaction. If we pause, and choose what we will do or say, then it is a response. For example, if someone offends you, your natural instinct might be to say something scathing back to them. But you do have the ability to choose. In the second before you speak, if you have trained yourself in self-control (especially in speech - see James chapter 3 in the Bible for this), then you can choose not to respond in kind, but choose a response that will calm the situation down rather than escalate it. The training in biblical character helps us to take advantage of those brief moments, and respond in a better way than sheer reaction.

The problem with discipline is that it does not sound like fun. And to be honest, at first it can be an uphill battle. But over time, it is the application of discipline that enables us to achieve things that were previously impossible for us. Through physically training our body in martial arts, we can learn to defeat a stronger, more powerful enemy, by knowing and applying superior techniques that have been grooved through sustained practice and discipline.

By training ourselves spiritually, we can develop a depth and quality of character that is beyond us right now. As the philosopher said, "The journey of a thousand miles begins with a single step." For

Christians, there are at least four major disciplines or habits that are essential for the effective Christian life: prayer, Bible study, Christian community, and service. We'll discuss those in detail shortly.

As an encouragement, I offer my own experience in attempting to spend a sustained time with God. I was scheduled to go on a retreat day, while working as a pastor for a church. You would think, since God is my everyday "business" that this would be easy for me, but it was not. I generally am easily bored and enjoy a lot of mental stimulation. I find it almost unbearable to be stuck somewhere, or delayed, and to have nothing to read. It's not an exaggeration to say that I was anticipating this day of retreat with a fair amount of dread.

The first part of the day, after the introduction, involved us going off for an hour and a half, without a Bible, notebook or anything else. We were supposed to find a quiet spot and pray. Even 90 minutes seemed like a long time to me, and at first, I wandered around the grounds, worried that God might not speak to me, and even more worried that perhaps God would speak to me, and have things to say that I was not anxious to hear! I expected to be frustrated, and what made it worse was the feeling that something had to happen, otherwise it would have been a complete waste of time. I felt a distinct pressure to hear from God, to prove that I had spiritual receptivity, to be "productive" even on this retreat day. Clearly there were some flaws in my thinking, and I think I was simply trying too hard. 30 minutes passed - nothing. 1 hour - nothing. It came to the last 15 minutes of the session, and I was stomping around frustrated, when I walked around a corner and saw a squirrel on the path. It did not see me, and carried on playfully running around the grass, scampering up and down a tree, and generally enjoying itself. As someone who spends most of his time inside, and living in the suburbs, I am still fascinated by nature, and this squirrel was putting on quite a show. We were down to the last 5 minutes or so before we had to get together and "report back" on anything God had said to us, when the spiritual significance of the squirrel became apparent to me. Either I was desperate to find some spiritual meaning anywhere, or perhaps God was really using the squirrel as an object lesson. In any case, this is what I thought. "I am enjoying this squirrel though he is completely unaware of my presence. There is no communication as such going on between us, but him just being there brings me joy." I wondered if it was the same between me and

God. Perhaps there hadn't been much in the way of communication, but maybe God could have joy simply from me being there in his presence, perhaps unaware of his presence, as the squirrel was of mine, but bringing him joy all the same."

I have to admit, it was with some relief that I could return to the group with my little squirrel story. My point is this: since that time I've been on a few retreats and I've learned some things that mean I no longer anticipate them with dread. In fact, often I quite look forward to creating space in my life where God can speak if he wishes. And to take the pressure off myself (which I think hinders my ability to listen), I tell myself that if, at the end of the day, the only result was that I was there for God's pleasure, then that is fine, and an acceptable use of the day. Usually, when I approach the day this way, it isn't long before I become aware of some areas God wishes to deal with me on, and I start writing them down, and the time flies.

In my case, and maybe in yours, it was the discipline to get beyond the first, extremely difficult experience, that has enabled it to be much easier now. Pushing through and seeing incremental improvements which over time create competency is far more the norm than something starting off easy and remaining so. Everything is difficult before it becomes easy.

One warning I have here - discipline at its best needs to be combined with passion, otherwise it can become cold and legalistic. We can easily move to a place of judging others who are not as disciplined as we are, and viewing them as inferior. In professional sports, the athlete practices the disciplines not for their own sake, but because they love the game and want to become more proficient in it. The lazy athlete who does not love the game will try and coast on raw talent. In our case, our embracing of the disciplines comes out of our passion to love God with our heart, mind, soul and strength, and to love others as we love ourselves. The disciplines are not an end in themselves, but the means to a glorious goal of a life of love.

Let's move on to consider some key disciplines of the Christian life.

Four Key Disciplines

PRAYER

Prayer is the lifeline for the Christian. Because of this, it is the area which is most often attacked by the enemy. If, to use military terminology, the enemy can cut off communications from HQ, the soldier will be left with a limited perspective, and forced to rely upon his own resources. Precisely for that reason, prayer must be a priority for the Christian. If they are honest, many Christians struggle with prayer. Studies have shown that 90% of people in the church do not have a praying life. Most people feel guilt, (I'm doing it badly, or not enough) confusion (I don't know how to do it) and frustration (it isn't working – my heart shuts down, becomes cynical). You may be in this 90% statistic. If you are, take heart. There are some simple steps to take, and a wealth of resources to consult, which can help you start to do better in this area.

We see the importance of prayer when we look at the life of Jesus. In fact, he went so far as to say that he was helpless without input from his Heavenly Father:

Jesus gave them this answer: "I tell you the truth, the Son can do nothing by himself; he can do only what he sees his Father doing, because whatever the Father does the Son also does." (John 5:19)

Many times in the gospels we see that Jesus holds up children as examples of how we should approach God. Have you noticed how children approach their parents with their requests? They are often unashamed. They boldly ask. They do not weigh up beforehand whether this is a reasonable or important request. They are persistent (another quality admired by Jesus) and they are convinced enough of their parents' love that they expect a positive response. This is entirely in keeping with how Jesus presents his Heavenly Father's attitude towards those who pray:

> 7 "Ask and it will be given to you; seek and you will find; knock and the door will be opened to you. 8 For everyone who asks receives; he who seeks finds; and to him who knocks, the door will be opened.
>
> 9 "Which of you, if his son asks for bread, will give him a stone? 10 Or if he asks for a fish, will give him a snake? 11 If you, then, though you are evil, know how to give good gifts

to your children, how much more will your Father in heaven give good gifts to those who ask him!" (Matthew 7:7-11)

As our starting point, we must begin with the idea that God loves us, delights to hear our requests and (assuming they are in keeping with his divine will) is more than willing to grant those requests. Our problems in prayer are perhaps twofold: either we do not ask (do we forget? Do we not believe God will answer?) or when we ask, we ask selfishly. James says it this way:

> "You do not have, because you do not ask God. 3 When you ask, you do not receive, because you ask with wrong motives, that you may spend what you get on your pleasures." (James 4:2b-3)

There's a balance to be had, a middle path, between bold asking, and avoiding selfishness. Paul Miller, in his excellent book, A Praying Life, talks about this in more detail, and offers the example of Jesus' prayer in the Garden of Gethsemane:

> "Abba, Father," he said, "everything is possible for you. Take this cup from me. Yet not what I will, but what you will." (Mark 14:36)

What we see there is a beautiful balance between bold asking (take this cup) and an utter lack of selfishness (yet not what I will, but what you will). To ask the cup of suffering to be removed is certainly a bold request. Jesus is not some type of inhuman superman who can face the agonizing ordeal of flogging and crucifixion without a shudder. If there is another way then, please God, let's go that way. But in his humility and submission, he places himself under the Father's will. That is an excellent pattern for our prayers. Ask boldly. Do not ask selfishly.

With that as an appropriate mindset and approach, let's look at a simple prayer pattern that many have found helpful, based on the acronym ACTS (Adoration, Confession, Thanksgiving, Supplication):

ADORATION: Begin the prayer by adoring God. Praise and worship HIM. This is a time for telling God what He means to you and how much you love Him. This is not the same as Thanksgiving where you thank God for all He has done, but a time to tell God how magnificent/holy/glorious He is, to focus solely on Him and the character qualities you admire in Him, to tell Him all the wondrous beautiful things about Him you love. King David was a great worshipper of God and God Himself stated that David was a man after His own heart. Read the Psalms for great examples of adoration e.g.:

> O Lord, our Lord,
>
> how majestic is your name in all the earth!
>
> You have set your glory
>
> above the heavens. (Psalm 8:1)

Hebrews 13:15 encourages us: "Through Jesus, therefore, let us continually offer to God a sacrifice of praise-the fruit of lips that confess his name."

CONFESSION: This is when we confess all our sins to God. Unconfessed sin can create a barrier between us and God, and can hinder our prayers. Begin by confessing your sin to Him with an apologetic and repentant heart (to repent is to stop and turn 180 degrees from). Ask God to bring to mind any sins you may not be aware of so you may repent and confess. "If we confess our sins, he is faithful and just and will forgive us our sins and purify us from all unrighteousness." (I John 1:8-9). Often times the feeling of a weight lifting will follow this step. Important: Nothing can separate you from the love of God. But we can separate ourselves from "sensing" the love of God just as Adam and Eve ran and hid from the Presence of God after their sin in the Garden. Notice God called after them; He did not wait for them to come to Him.

THANKSGIVING: This is where we count our blessings, thanking and praising God for all He has given us and done for us in life. You may begin with the basics such as family, friends, food, shelter, safety, jobs, health and healing. Thank Him for hearing your prayers and for forgiving your sins, for His all-consuming love for you. Thank Him for His promises, for the glory of His handiwork, for His promises to you (if you don't know them, start looking them up). Follow Paul's advice in Ephesians 5:20 "…giving thanks always for all things unto God and the Father in the name of our Lord Jesus Christ."

SUPPLICATION: This is also known as Intercession. This is the phase of prayer where we come to the Father asking God to supply needs for ourselves and others. Be specific in your prayers. For example, instead of asking for God to bless your family, ask Him to help your son focus in math class and to give his teacher the wisdom she needs to present the information in a way he can digest, etc. If you feel led to pray for a certain person but don't know exactly what that person needs, ask God to lead you in prayer. He will.

Remember, prayer is an act of communing with God. It is about communication. It is about relationship with the Father. Use these steps to help you obtain that but don't feel you must adhere to any rigid rules. Also don't forget that communication is a two-way street, which means you have to listen as well. You may not hear at first but with practice you begin to feel God speaking to your heart.

Some other tips that may help you as you begin to develop the discipline of prayer:

- try writing down your prayers. This is great for two reasons. Firstly, it helps you avoid distractions and a wandering mind. Secondly, it provides a record of what you have asked God for, and you can look back and see his faithfulness in answering your prayers, which will spur you on to pray even more boldly and confidently.
- try saying your prayers out loud. There's something about verbalizing a prayer, rather than just thinking it through in your mind, which makes it feel more serious and heartfelt. You may feel strange doing this at first, but it will soon feel normal.
- speak normally to God. Don't try and use clever theological phrases, King James English (thou knowest, O Lord, mine needs, and I beseecheth thee...) - just be normal. God understands your heart and is not impressed with showy, impressive prayers. Heartfelt, sincere, authentic prayers are of greater value than eloquent ones.

BIBLE READING

In preparing for my last Tae Kwondo training, I had to revisit the training manual I had been given, to refresh my memory on various Korean terms, and the number of moves in the different forms. In the same way, the Bible has been given to us as a training manual, and we ignore it at our peril.

Apart from the person of Jesus Christ, the clearest way in which

God has chosen to reveal himself to humanity is through the Bible. There have been many books written about how the Bible was compiled, and why it can be trusted, but that is beyond this small book. I will take it as read that the reader believes the Bible is inspired by God, and as such, is the true guide to life and every aspect of Christian behavior.

Again, because the Word of God is so important to the Christian, it is another area of attack for the enemy. If he can stop us from reading God's revelation to us in the Bible, then he can prevent us from seeing the world, and ourselves, as God sees them. In the end, it is God's perspective that counts, and the more we read the Bible, the more we align ourselves with his view of things. For example, much of the world counts success in monetary terms, whereas the Bible counts success as a life lived with character and integrity. Which view of success are we going to align ourselves with?

In many ways, the world sings to us a siren song of warped values and priorities, and it is only by clinging to the mast of God's truth that we can avoid the peril of those rocks.

Many people are put off studying the Bible because it is an intimidating book. For a start, it is massive. It contains 66 books written by about 40 different authors, in varying types (or genres) of literature, ranging from narrative (like the gospels, fairly easy to understand) to the apocalyptic (like Revelation, much more difficult) with other types like poetry, wisdom literature, psalms, proverbs and history all bundled together in there. No wonder a beginning reader can feel intimidated.

Many people in trying to read the Bible start at the beginning, and make their way pretty well through Genesis and Exodus but come to a screeching halt in Leviticus, which is full of arcane laws and rules about life, almost all of which do not pertain directly to us today.

My recommendation if you are new to the Bible, is that you start at the beginning of the New Testament rather than the Old Testament. The gospels, Matthew, Mark, Luke and John, are far easier to comprehend, and also introduce you directly to Jesus who is, let's face it, the core person of the faith. The Old Testament Law, prophecies, and history in many ways foreshadow what is fulfilled in Jesus Christ, his sacrificial death on the cross, his resurrection from the dead, and the founding of the church.

There are many ways to study the Bible. I'll list just a few:

- overview - reading some extracts from different books
- character study - studying the life of a biblical character such as David, or Saul/Paul
- book study - studying the Bible one book at a time
- thematic study - following a theme, like holiness, through the Bible

and many more.

For now, I'm going to teach you a simple way of approaching the Scriptures that should have an immediate benefit. It follows the acronym S.O.A.P., which stands for Scripture, Observation, Application, Prayer. An easy way to remember is to think about your life being washed by the Word, with **SOAP**.

S - Scripture. Read the passage of Scripture you have chosen. Don't make it too long. Make sure it's not so much that you can't hold the main idea(s) in your head.

O - Observation. What does the passage actually say? Be careful not to make it say what you want it to say, but read it in a straightforward way. What is going on here? Why does the writer say this? Who is he writing to? What are their issues? What does he recommend or command? If it's a story about Jesus, what is happening? Why did the author choose to include this story? What does it reveal about God/Jesus/the Holy Spirit? What does it reveal about humankind?

A - Application. What lessons are to be learned from this? Is there a sin to be avoided, or some action to emulate or incorporate into my own life. Is there an attitude or value that is challenged or promoted? What lesson can I apply to my own life here? How would that look?

P - Prayer. Take a few minutes to pray this through. Ask God to help you make the change you have observed, or adjust your life to more closely match what he wants.

As an example of how SOAP would work in practice, let's look at the story of the Rich Young Ruler, found in the gospel of Mark:

17 As Jesus started on his way, a man ran up to him and fell on his knees before him. "Good teacher," he asked, "what must I do to inherit eternal life?"

18 "Why do you call me good?" Jesus answered. "No one is good--except God alone. 19 You know the commandments: 'Do not murder, do not commit adultery, do not steal, do not give false testimony, do not defraud, honor your father and mother.'"

20 "Teacher," he declared, "all these I have kept since I was a boy."

21 Jesus looked at him and loved him. "One thing you lack," he said. "Go, sell everything you have and give to the poor, and you will have treasure in heaven. Then come, follow me."

22 At this the man's face fell. He went away sad, because he had great wealth.

23 Jesus looked around and said to his disciples, "How hard it is for the rich to enter the kingdom of God!"

24 The disciples were amazed at his words. But Jesus said again, "Children, how hard it is to enter the kingdom of God! 25 It is easier for a camel to go through the eye of a needle than for a rich man to enter the kingdom of God."

26 The disciples were even more amazed, and said to each other, "Who then can be saved?"

27 Jesus looked at them and said, "With man this is impossible, but not with God; all things are possible with God." (Mark 10:17-27)

Let's use SOAP to analyze this passage.

S - Scripture. We just read it. Moving on...

O - Observation. What is happening here? Jesus is approached by a man who is interested in gaining eternal life, and asks him how to do it. Jesus replies with some of the commandments which the man says he has kept since he was young. Jesus then tells him to sell everything he owns and give it to the poor, then follow him. The man is unwilling to do this since he is very rich. Jesus tells the crowd that it is hard for rich people to enter the kingdom of heaven.

A - Application. Here are some of the potential applications of this passage:
- Jesus wants us to obey the commandments, but may require more of us. What more might Jesus require of me?
- Wealth was a barrier to this man following Jesus. Is there any barrier in my life that could hinder me following Jesus? What should I do about it?
- The rich might find it hard to enter the kingdom of heaven because they tend to trust in their wealth rather than God. Am I placing my trust in something other than God? How can I more clearly demonstrate my trust in God?
- God wants all people, rich and poor to be saved. Is there anyone I've written off? Do I need to revise my view, bearing in mind that "all things are possible with God?"
- Am I living as though all things are possible with God, or am I living as though God is restricted? Is there something bold I need to pray for?

P - Prayer. This could be a sample prayer after thinking this through. "God, I want to follow you with my whole heart. Show me if there is anything hindering this whole-hearted devotion to you. If there is something, show me what to do about it. I want to be obedient to you, and do all that you ask of me. With you all things are possible. Use me for your purposes, and help me grow in my love and obedience of you."

In terms of resources available to you, if you have access to the internet, a world of possibilities is open. One of the best is a site called YouVersion: https://www.youversion.com/

The site has many translations of the Bible, but perhaps the most valuable resource is the Bible reading plans. Here is a summary of some that are currently offered:

The One Year ® Bible, 1 Year
Experience the insights and joy gained from reading the entire

Bible. You can do it in as little as 15 minutes a day with The One Year ® Bible, the world's most popular annual reading Bible. Daily readings from the Old Testament, New Testament, Psalms, and Proverbs will guide you through God's Word in one year.

Life Application Study Bible ® Devotion, 1 Year

Learn to apply God's Word more fully in your life with the Life Application Study Bible ® Devotion. Each day you will receive a brief devotional featuring a Scripture verse and note taken from the Life Application Study Bible ® designed to help you apply the Bible to your life.

Prayer, 3 Weeks

Learn how best to pray, both from the prayers of the faithful and from the words of Jesus Himself. Find encouragement to keep taking your requests to God every day, with persistence and patience. Explore examples of empty, self-righteous prayers, balanced against the pure prayers of those with clean hearts. Pray constantly.

The Gospels, 30 Days

This plan, compiled and presented by the folks at YouVersion.com, will help you read through all four Gospels in thirty days. Get a firm grasp of Jesus' life and ministry in a short span of time.

Psalms and Proverbs in 31 Days, 31 Days

The Psalms and Proverbs are filled with songs, poetry, and writings expressing true worship, longing, wisdom, love, desperation, and truth. This plan will take you through all of the Psalms and Proverbs in just 31 days. Here, you will encounter God and find comfort, strength, solace, and encouragement that covers the breadth of the human experience.

Thirty-One Days of Healing & Recovery, 31 Days

The idea that God wants you well is both exciting and controversial. Opinions and theological positions are many and the debate has raged on for years. Thirty-One Days of Healing & Recovery is a compilation of short healing passages and verses that you can read every day for a month. The purpose is to allow the scriptures to form and/or strengthen your beliefs as to the ability and willingness of God to heal today.

ReThink Life: 40 Day Devotional, 40 Days

Most people approach life based on what popular culture says is normal, but when we approach life from God's perspective it changes everything. This 40-Day ReThink Life Experiment is based upon Rodney and Michelle Gage's new book called ReThink Life. This experiment will challenge you to "rethink" seven of the most important areas of life. Each day focuses on a verse of scripture, key thought, and prayer for the day. To learn more about the book and other free resources please visit www.rethinklife.com.

The Essential 100, 100 days

The Essential 100 Challenge (E100) helps you get an overview of the Bible... without getting bogged down. The Plan guides you through 50 Old Testament passages and 50 New Testament passages -- The Essential 100 -- so you can see the big picture of God's Word, and form a daily Bible reading habit in the process. E100 is an achievable way to have a "through the Bible" experience; it's the Bible reading plan people love to complete.

Bible reading plans like this are an incredibly valuable resource. You can also connect the program/website to your Facebook account, to let your friends know what (and how often!) you are reading. That in itself can help you be consistent, as studies have shown that social "pressure" can help people significantly in developing new habits.

It is inevitable that at some point in your Bible reading you will encounter a word or verse that is confusing to you. In fact, the meaning of a whole section might be somewhat murky or unclear. In such situations, a good commentary is very useful. A commentary is simply a book containing explanatory notes about the Bible. Some of them are single book commentaries (e.g. A commentary on the Gospel of Mark) while some commentaries cover the whole Bible. A very good online resource is SonicLight, written by Dr. Constable, who is a conservative scholar with an excellent reputation. You can access the study notes section of his website here: http://www.soniclight.com/constable/notes.htm though the whole site is worth checking out.

For a single volume commentary that is not too expensive, I recommend The New Bible Commentary by InterVarsityPress.

Also recommended as a companion purchase is a Bible Dictionary, such as The New Bible Dictionary, also published by IVP.

For a little under $60 you can have resources that will answer 95% of your Bible questions. For the other 5%, go bother your pastor!

The last resource I will mention is Living by the Book, by Howard Hendricks. "In a simple, step-by-step fashion, the authors explain how to glean truth from Scripture. It is practical, readable, and applicable. By following its easy-to-apply principles, you'll soon find yourself drawing great nourishment from the Word-and enjoying the process! The Living by the Book Workbook is the perfect complement to provide practical application of lessons."

Once you get into reading the Bible, and seeing its relevance to your life, it's very compelling. Even though you may wonder what a 2000 year old (and much older) book has to do with your life, bear in mind that over the centuries, human character has not changed very much, and God has not changed at all. The passions, fears, pursuits, obsessions, loves, hates of humankind do not alter much. You may be surprised, in reading the Bible, at how well God seems to know you, and how similar (uncomfortably so, sometimes) we are to those who have gone before.

CHRISTIAN COMMUNITY

I have found, in martial arts training, that I am much more likely to push myself to excellence if I am training with others. If I train on my own, I can be easily discouraged, or become tired, and if there is no one to push me to do one more form, twenty more push-ups, twenty more sit-ups... then I can be tempted to take it easy or even give up. You can do it on your own, but it's much better, and much more effective, if you train with others.

In the same way, as mentioned earlier, the Christian life was not designed to be a solitary pursuit. We are supposed to be part of a faith community, in which we can be encouraged and challenged by others, and do our own fair share of encouraging and challenging also. At the basic level, we need to be part of a church. I have heard people from time to time say that they have no need for organized religion, or a formal church setting. They say they can just as easily worship God through nature, or listening to music, or studying art. I don't buy it. Generally there is a reason why these people are avoiding community, and it's not a healthy one. They prefer religion on their terms, often devoid of challenge, and so steer clear of any place where that might happen. A forest is not going to ask you why you are so angry despite claiming to have the Prince of Peace ruling in your heart. A person at church probably would.

Beyond regular church attendance, being part of a smaller group is a vital Christian discipline. On our own, we are vulnerable to attack from the enemy, or even our own idiosyncratic interpretations of the Bible or how to live out the Christian life. It is like coals in a fire. When they are all clustered together, warmth is maintained. But when one falls out onto the hearth, it soon grows cold. I have seen it time and time again, that a Christian who withdraws from community is soon on a downward spiral which will end in a lifestyle that denies Christ.

One of the great tactics of the enemy is to isolate Christians, to get them to the point where they feel that their issues are unique, and that no one else feels like them. A pity party is the Devil's playground. In a small group however, if you are prepared to be vulnerable, you can be truly known for who you are, and find that you are loved all the same. In the best of groups, we know others deeply, and we are known deeply ourselves. In that environment, we can feel safe to be honest about our struggles and find accountability which will help us grow as a disciple of Jesus Christ. It is one thing to hear a sermon about anger, for example. It is quite another level to confess to a friend in a small group, that you struggle with this, and would he ask you how you are doing in this area next week? Suddenly discipleship has become practical, accountability is in place, and real life change is a whole lot closer.

A word of warning: don't expect your small group to be perfect. A small group is full of sinners, of which you are one! It is precisely in these environments of imperfection where someone is annoying, where someone offends you, where someone is excessively needy, that the real, genuine Christian "work" of love, forgiveness and perseverance can be put into practice. The German theologian, Dietrich Bonhoeffer in his book Life Together, said that Christian community is designed to be disappointing. If it were not, we would be tempted to worship community rather than God himself.

Most churches offer small groups, and see them as a vital component of discipleship. Contact yours and ask how you can get connected to one. Most groups would be happy to have you visit and see if you like the members of the group, and the format of their meetings. Take the bold step and join one. It is a way to truly accelerate your discipleship, to be around those who may be further along in the faith, who can take you under their wing, and help you learn from the mistakes they made, rather than you learning from your own.

SERVING

One of the first things I learned to do at the start of a martial arts training session is bow. In the UK, we bowed to the instructor. In the US, we bow to the US Flag, and then the instructor. In both cases, it is a reminder of status. We are according respect to something (or someone) greater than our individual selves. In bowing to the flag we recognize our allegiance and loyalty to our country. In bowing to our instructor, we acknowledge his or her superior skills, and our dependence on them for learning.

As a Christian, our humility is demonstrated in a different way. Of course we should respect and honor others, but a key marker of maturity in a growing disciple is their willingness to serve; to offer their skills and abilities to something greater than themselves. In practical terms, this usually means volunteering in the church, or for some worthy organization like Habitat for Humanity.

The perfect example of a life of service is the life of Jesus himself. Although, as God come in the flesh, he would have been perfectly justified in having humanity serve him, he saw it as his role to serve humanity:

"For even the Son of Man did not come to be served, but to serve, and to give his life as a ransom for many." (Mark 10:45)

The apostle Paul, in writing about Jesus Christ in the book of Philippians, emphasized his servant nature:

"Each of you should look not only to your own interests, but also to the interests of others.

5 Your attitude should be the same as that of Christ Jesus:
6 Who, being in very nature God,

did not consider equality with God something to be grasped,
7 but made himself nothing,
taking the very nature of a servant,..." (Philippians 2:4b-7)

We see this attitude in practice in John chapter 13, when Jesus washes his disciple's feet:

"Having loved his own who were in the world, he now showed them the full extent of his love.

2 The evening meal was being served, and the devil had already prompted Judas Iscariot, son of Simon, to betray Jesus. 3 Jesus knew that the Father had put all things under his power, and that he had come from God and was returning to God; 4 so he got up from the meal, took off his outer clothing, and wrapped a towel around his waist. 5 After that, he poured water into a basin and began to wash his disciples' feet, drying them with the towel that was wrapped around him.
6 He came to Simon Peter, who said to him, "Lord, are you going to wash my feet?"
7 Jesus replied, "You do not realize now what I am doing, but later you will understand."
8 "No," said Peter, "you shall never wash my feet." (John 13:2-8)

Peter is so shocked by this action that he tries to prevent Jesus from washing his feet.

One of the chief characteristics demonstrated here is humility. Proud people tend not to serve others. The Bible is very clear that God opposes the proud and that humility is a virtue to be cultivated. Serving others is a great way to do this.

According to the Bible, each Christian has been given a spiritual gift, that is some special talent or ability, that can be used for building up the church and being a blessing to others. For some people, this gift is very apparent. For others, some research and trial and error may be required.

In my own case, I had the benefit of both approaches. The pastor at the church where I became a Christian taught for a whole year, on

Sunday evenings, on the subject of spiritual gifts. These sermons were both informational and inspirational. They created a hunger in me to find out what my own spiritual gift was, and to try and use that to bless others. You may or may not have a church that is interested in helping you discover your own spiritual gifts. Ideally this is something you would want to do as part of a group, so that others can see and affirm your gifting, or if necessary, set you straight if you are in error. Sometimes the truth is that we wish we were gifted in something, but it is apparent to everyone around us that that really is not our gift. A true friend will let us know that, and steer us towards areas in which we might be more effective.

If you are investigating this on your own, there are a number of spiritual gift tests online which can help you discern how God has wired you to be of service to others. You can do a Google search with the keywords "spiritual gifts" or try some of the links below:

http://www.churchgrowth.org/cgi-cg/gifts.cgi?intro=1
http://www.kodachrome.org/spiritgift/
http://mintools.com/spiritual-gifts-test.htm

These online tests are free, but there are also some excellent books that can give you a more in-depth idea of your gifting:

- Understanding Spiritual Gifts by Kay Arthur, David Lawson, B.J. Lawson
- What You Do Best in the Body of Christ: Discover Your Spiritual Gifts, Personal Style, and God-Given Passion by Bruce L. Bugbee
- Discover Your Spiritual Gifts: Identify and Understand Your Unique God-Given Spiritual Gifts by C. Peter Wagner Ph.D.

Once you have a basic idea of your gifts, you need to get involved in some ministries at your church and test them out. If it is a genuine spiritual gift you can expect that your gifting will be affirmed by others, and that you personally should gain some degree of satisfaction from exercising this gift. If it is not affirmed, or you don't find serving in this area of ministry satisfying, then perhaps you need to revisit the question of whether this really is one of your spiritual gifts.

A church functioning at its best is a bit like an orchestra. Each person fulfills their own unique role, and together they create a symphony of service which blesses others and honors God. So here are the steps you need to take, to begin a life of service:
1. Ask your Christian friends what gifts or abilities they see in you, that could be of service to God or the wider world.
2. Complete a spiritual gifts test online and/or buy one of the books recommended above and work through it.
3. Once you have a sense of how you may be gifted, speak to a pastor, or the person in charge of volunteering/serving at your church, and say you would like to get involved and try some things.
4. Assess how effective you are in the chosen area of service. Ask others to give you honest feedback. It may take a few attempts before you find a great fit, but when you do, it will be thrilling to see how God can use you to serve and bless others.

Lastly, some warnings. Don't start to see yourself as better than other Christians who may not be serving. Pride is always a trap for the unwary. Try to avoid comparison and judging others. Secondly, don't imagine that God loves you more or less because you serve. He loves you simply because you are his child, not for how you perform, or serve him. Third, monitor your resources. Ideally your service should overflow from your life together with God. If you do it in your own strength, and do not have a good sense of boundaries or your own limits, you can end up being burned out and resentful. If this starts to happen, then take a break, and come back later with a renewed sense of energy and enthusiasm.

4. BE AWARE - EVIL IS OUT THERE

There have been two situations in real life where I have been called upon to use my martial arts training. Once to help someone else, and once to defend myself against an attack.

The first situation happened when I was working in Folkestone, a town in the South of England. I was walking back from lunch, towards my office, when I saw a man grabbing a girl by the wrist and dragging her along the pavement, in a way that it was clear she did not want to go. As I looked closer, I saw that he had her in a wrist-lock, similar to one I had learned in Jiu-Jitsu. I assessed my options. As a chivalrous Englishman, I could not simply ignore a damsel in distress. Since this was England and not America, there was a very small chance that the man was armed with a weapon. I could have confronted him, but if I did that, I would remove the element of surprise which could work to my advantage. So, finally, after that split-second review of options, I walked up on his blind side, the opposite side from where he was holding the girl, and grabbed his wrist with the same wrist-lock, but I applied it with significantly more force. He shouted out in pain, released the girl, and I told her to run (in case he managed to escape my grip). As it happened, I had a pretty good hold on him, which I made even stronger by adding my other hand, which left him only able to move in the direction I wished. With him still gripped in this painful wrist-lock, I marched him back to my office, which was about 50 yards away, and told my secretary to call the police. They came, took charge of the situation, and all ended well. This was a situation I decided to get involved in. I could have ignored it and walked away, but that would have been wrong. I think we have a moral responsibility, as men, as Christians, and even simply as humans, to defend those who are being bullied, and are unable to defend themselves.

The next situation was not one of choice. I was working in Berlin as a missionary, and walking with my team through a square called Alexanderplatz, on the former East side of the Wall. As we were walking, I noticed a group of men sitting on a bench, who from their demeanor and loud voices had clearly been drinking. I glanced at them briefly (they were hard to ignore) and something about my look, or simply me being there, seemed to irk one of these guys. This huge man-mountain, almost certainly a body builder from the size of his muscles, walked over to me, grabbed my right hand and placed it on his shirt. He then grabbed my shirt with his left hand, and started to swing at me. I realized that he had, without my agreement, involved me in a slug-fest, which presumably would only end when one of us dropped unconscious to the floor. Before I had time to argue, or extol the virtues of peaceful conflict resolution, he was swinging a hefty right arm at me. Quickly I threw up my left arm in a forearm block, and effectively stopped his blow before it made violent contact with my face. He then paused for a moment, probably expecting me to take my turn at hitting him, but I didn't want any part of this game. Not satisfied with my passive approach, he swung again, and again and again. Each time, I blocked him, and I could tell he was getting frustrated that he couldn't hit me.

It was strange, but even in the midst of this frantic activity, it seemed like part of me was separate, observing the situation and working out how best to end it. I could knee him in the groin, but I had the sneaking suspicion that his fellow body-builders would see this as unfair, and join in the fray. I was fairly confident about handling one, but seven or eight would definitely be too many. As I was still thinking it over, he swung a blow so hard, and I blocked it so strongly, that his watch strap snapped, and his watch went flying. He walked over to retrieve his watch, and I applied the first law of jiu-jitsu and seized this moment to run away.

As a Christian we will be faced by both types of situations. Sometimes we will actively seek out evil, or the effects of evil, and sometimes we will just come across it.

It is important to recognize that evil is internal as well as external. None of us like to think of ourselves as evil. Perhaps it is better to say that we sometimes have evil tendencies, which sometimes translate into evil words and deeds. The error we must avoid is to think that there is no evil in ourselves, that it is just external, or just someone else's problem. If you've ever listened to a sermon, and thought to yourself, "This person should have heard this sermon" while failing to see how it applied to you, you may be prone to this tendency.

Alexander Solzhenitsyn made this point clear with this quote:

> "Gradually it was disclosed to me that the line separating good and evil passes not through states, nor between classes, nor between political parties either, but right through every human heart, and through all human hearts. This line shifts. Inside us, it oscillates with the years. Even within hearts overwhelmed by evil, one small bridgehead of good is retained; and even in the best of all hearts, there remains a small corner of evil... If only there were evil people somewhere insidiously committing evil deeds, and it were necessary only to separate them from the rest of us and destroy them. But the line dividing good and evil cuts through the heart of every human being. And who is willing to destroy a piece of his own heart?"

While external evils are real, and must be resisted, it is the evil in our own hearts that we must face first. Severe honesty, and accountability relationships where we are willing to confess the worst of ourselves to another, are keys to resisting this temptation to see ourselves as better than others, and less prone to sin.

Once we have worked at purifying our own hearts, then we are better placed to combat the external evils that surround us. This is a brief, and by no means exclusive list.

MATERIALISM/GREED

In a world that keeps score by money and possessions, this is a powerful temptation. We are seduced into locating our worth and value by what we own or earn. When I became a Christian, this was the first area God dealt with me on, because up to that point, I had been breathlessly pursuing wealth, and the status that normally tags along with it. In fact, my pursuit of wealth, and concern over finances were significant barriers to trusting in a God who promises that he knows our needs and will take care of us. As I get older as a Christian, I have more of a track record of God's faithful provision to rely on, but still the temptation rears its ugly head from time to time and needs to be put down.

CONSUMER MENTALITY

In much of the Western world we are viewed, and tend to identify ourselves, as consumers. When you consider the vast amount of money spent on advertising, and how much time we spend thinking about our "needs" which are more often "wants" we can see how easy it is to fall into this trap. This is connected to the temptation of materialism and greed of course, but also has a sinister aspect when we import our consumer mentality into the church. It doesn't take long before we decide that we have certain preferences, that we want things "our way." "Have it your way" may work well in Burger King, but it is an unhealthy and unhelpful attitude to bring into the church. Before long, we can start to see church as a place to satisfy our needs and preferences, rather than a place to carry our cross, serve the body of Christ, and submit ourselves to leadership. How many churches have split not over serious doctrinal issues, but over trivialities such as music style, or even the color of the church carpet? However your consumer mentality expresses itself in normal life, you would be well advised to check it at the door of the church, and come with a heart that is open to worshiping God in any style, and hearing from him through any means.

SEXUAL IMMORALITY

Perhaps the strongest trap for the young Christian, though even for the more mature in the faith, the temptation may remain ever present, whether it is the allure of sex outside of marriage, or the illicit world of internet pornography. When I first came to faith I was 20 years old, and there was certainly a challenge to remain pure and godly, while all the time the late teen/early twenties hormones were raging. No one is immune. There is no shortage of pastors who have fallen from grace through engaging in sexual immorality. It seems to be something against which we need to be perpetually on guard. My recommendation is to build walls of defense against falling. Install anti-porn software on your computer, something that will block access to adult sites. Consider signing up to xxxchurch.com and installing software that reports your suspicious web browsing to a trusted friend of your choice. Have an accountability partner who will ask you direct questions about sexual purity, and promise never to lie. (Choose this partner carefully - it must be a person who shows grace, but who also has enough backbone to hold you accountable when/if you fall. It should also be a person of the utmost discretion who you can trust to keep your confessions confidential.

5. WITH GREAT POWER COMES GREAT RESPONSIBILITY

There is a saying that with great power comes great responsibility. I remember being amazed, after a few months of training, at the terrible destructive power that was now within my grasp. I could, quite literally, kill someone with what I knew, or at least seriously damage them to the point where they would need a visit to the hospital. We learned early on in training to hold back on our power, and the severity with which we would apply wrist and arm-locks. If we had used full power, there would have been serious injuries.

I suffered one once, when a person threw me with a lock on. They were not really experienced enough to do this, and I didn't know how to react to it. As it was, I got off lightly with a hyper-extended elbow - but that was a doctor visit, and it could just have easily been a broken arm.

What was taught to me then, and something that is a pillar of Tae

Kwondo (my current martial art) is the importance of self-control. We learned to exercise self-control in practice, but we also learned to exercise it in real life. You certainly become more cautious about getting involved in a fight when you know the damage you can do. You want to be sure that it really merits your involvement, because the consequences to the other person are likely to be serious.

The Bible has plenty of exhortations to self-control. It is a fruit of the Spirit (Galatians 5:22-23):

> 22 But the fruit of the Spirit is love, joy, peace, forbearance, kindness, goodness, faithfulness, 23 gentleness and self-control.

The Book of Proverbs has a serious warning:

> 32 Better a patient person than a warrior,
> one with self-control than one who takes a city. (Proverbs 16:32)

This is a direct challenge to the mentality of martial artists, who like to think of ourselves as warriors. In God's sight, a personality that exhibits self-control is better than having the fighting ability to take a city. Better a person with self-control than Rambo!

> 28 Like a city whose walls are broken through
> is a person who lacks self-control. (Proverbs 25:28)

And here:

> 3 It is God's will that you should be sanctified: that you should avoid sexual immorality; 4 that each of you should learn to control your own body in a way that is holy and honorable, 5 not in passionate lust like the pagans, who do not know God; (1 Thessalonians 4:3-5)

In the small letter of Titus, self-control is a dominant theme:

> You, however, must teach what is appropriate to sound doctrine. 2 Teach the older men to be temperate, worthy of respect, self-controlled, and sound in faith, in love and in endurance.
> 3 Likewise, teach the older women to be reverent in the way they live, not to be slanderers or addicted to much wine, but

to teach what is good. 4 Then they can urge the younger women to love their husbands and children, 5 to be self-controlled and pure, to be busy at home, to be kind, and to be subject to their husbands, so that no one will malign the word of God.

6 Similarly, encourage the young men to be self-controlled. (Titus 2:1-6)

11 For the grace of God has appeared that offers salvation to all people. 12 It teaches us to say "No" to ungodliness and worldly passions, and to live self-controlled, upright and godly lives in this present age, 13 while we wait for the blessed hope--the appearing of the glory of our great God and Savior, Jesus Christ. (Titus 2:11-13)

The apostle Peter also points out its importance:

5 For this very reason, make every effort to add to your faith goodness; and to goodness, knowledge; 6 and to knowledge, self-control; and to self-control, perseverance; and to perseverance, godliness; 7 and to godliness, mutual affection; and to mutual affection, love. (2 Peter 1:5-7)

The challenge for us as Christians, as well as martial artists, is to lead self-controlled lives. Just as we take pride in our ability to control our body, and unleash amazing force if required, we should work equally hard at controlling our temper, our responses and our reactions, so that they can be self-controlled and pleasing to God.

6 THE POWER IN PERSEVERANCE

In my own recent belt test, I had come back to the sport after a period of many years absence. I was working on regaining my fitness, but hadn't really done so by the time of the test. For me it was a matter of gritting my teeth and working through the pain of protesting muscles and laboring lungs. I did it, but I was about ready to drop at the end.

The Christian life is not easy. The challenge to pick up your cross daily is not a gentle invitation, but a call to a life radically devoted to Jesus Christ. There will be opposition and struggle, from other people, and especially from the enemy of our souls, Satan. The call to the Christian is not to give up. Give no ground to the enemy. Give him no reason to celebrate and crow about a victory over you. Remain loyal to your Lord and Master Jesus Christ, and persevere to the very end.

> 12 For our struggle is not against flesh and blood, but against the rulers, against the authorities, against the powers of this dark world and against the spiritual forces of evil in the heavenly realms. 13 Therefore put on the full armor of God, so that when the day of evil comes, you may be able to stand your ground, and after you have done everything, to stand. (Ephesians 6:12-13)

Do you notice what you get to do when you have done everything? Rest? Relax? No. Stand. Continue firm in the faith.

Continue serving the one who gave everything for you. Continue beating down the Devil wherever and whenever he raises his head. And when you have done all that, stand. Stand and receive the victor's welcome. Stand and receive the commendation of the Lord, who will, in the end say to you, "Well done, my good and faithful servant!"

AMAZON REVIEWS

Dear Reader,

If you found this book helpful, would you please do me a huge favor and write a brief review on Amazon.com. One or two sentences would be fine.

Here's the link to the page:

http://www.amazon.com/Martial-Taught-Gospel-Christ-ebook/dp/B00BP0S0TM

My hope is for the message of this book to be shared as widely as possible, and your review will help.

Also by Glyn Norman

If God Had a Fridge, Your Picture Would Be On It –
Self-Image: How Seeing Yourself as God Sees You Changes Everything

Our self-image is shaped by a number of sources: our family, society, what we have done, and what has been done to us. It is much like being in a carnival house of mirrors: at every turn we are presented with a distorted image of ourselves.

This book examines these sources of self-image and compares them to what God says about us and who we are. By looking at relevant Bible texts, you will gain a fresh perspective on the value God places on you and your potential.

From the Author:

"How many of us suffer in our relationships, in our view of ourselves and our potential, because we have been presented with a distorted image?

Maybe a parent made you feel unloved and unwanted.
Maybe a teacher convinced you that you would never amount to anything.
Perhaps a boss let you know how little he thought of you.
Maybe you have been abused and sinned against, and you feel dirty and ashamed.
Perhaps a spouse has chipped away at your self-belief and you feel like a failure.
Perhaps the weight of your own mistakes and poor choices weighs on you daily.
Maybe you became persuaded that if you were just a little prettier, a little smarter, a little less socially awkward, then you would be acceptable.

Over the years I have been a pastor, through hundreds of counseling appointments and pastoral conversations, I have seen the same issues surface again and again, with a common root cause: we look to the wrong places for our self-image.

Only when we understand how God sees us will we experience freedom. Understanding how we appear to God changes everything. Only when we appreciate to the depths of our being, how precious and loved we are by our Creator and Savior, can we truly move into the abundant life that he promised us.

In this book, I examine the different sources of our self-image and will show you that you have a unique value to God, and a special place in his plan. As the title says, "If God had a fridge, your picture would be on it!"

FREE FIRST CHAPTER ON NEXT PAGE:

WHAT MARTIAL ARTS TAUGHT ME ABOUT THE GOSPEL OF JESUS CHRIST

Chapter One:
Does Anybody Even Want Me here?

Setting the Scene

I was 14 years old, sitting in the classroom waiting for class to start. One of the popular boys in class, Philip, was due to leave town the next week, moving with his parents to a far-off city in the north of England. The others in the "cool" group were gathered around him, because he was sharing his new address with those who wanted to write to him. I sat a few rows away, and also wrote down the address. We hadn't been the closest of friends, but I thought I might want to write.

Suddenly, one of the cool kids turned around, pointed at me and said, "Look, Half-Pint is writing it down." How they laughed. How they laughed at the very idea that their cool friend might want to get a letter from me, or even more hilarious, that he might want to write back. My face suffused with red shame, and I quietly put my pen and paper away. How foolish of me. How awkward and silly and embarrassing for me to dare count myself among his friends. I didn't show much expression, but inside I was crushed.

I realized that "Half-Pint" did not belong in this circle. That nickname was given to me because of my diminutive size (my body took a time out from growing at age 10 and didn't start up again until I was 13), and was just one of many that they used. Suffice it to say, I got the message. What was clearly reflected back to me was that I didn't belong. I had a social status, but it was far below that of these cool ones.

I don't make it a habit to watch scary films, but from my childhood, I think I remember more than one with a plot along these lines ...

A couple become stranded as their car runs out of fuel on a lonely forest road. They seek shelter at a Gothic mansion, where the door is opened by an old, old man who is willing to let them stay there for the night. As they make their way up the stairs to their room, the man issues a dire warning:

"Just one thing I ask ... whatever you do, do not go into the West Wing. There are things there ..." he never completes his sentence, his utterance seeming to have tired him. He waves his arm twice toward the stairway in dismissal and wanders down a dark corridor to his own room.

With trepidation, the couple ascends the stairs, finds their rooms and prepare for bed, though neither feels particularly sleepy after the dire warning.

And you, dear reader, know how the story continues. Foolishly, they do not heed the old man's advice. They hear noises and wander off to investigate the source, ending up in the West Wing, where they discover the old man's hideously deformed relative, whom he keeps hidden from the world. They run and trip as the drooling maniac stumbles toward them, his zombie-like gait never slowing ... you get the picture.

The message of this book is simply this: you are not the hideously deformed relative in the house that needs to be hidden away. You are not the one who slipped in, hoping your entrance wouldn't get noticed, while all the good people were being admitted. You are not the sum of the opinions, judgments, criticisms, sarcasm, looks and comments of others. You are not the sum of your parents, your education, your job, society or any other source.

For most of us, our self-image is like what we see when we walk through a hall of mirrors. At every turn, a different version of ourselves is reflected back to us: thinner, fatter, distorted. In a carnival, it is funny - in life, it is tragic. We find ourselves compromised in our ability to love ourselves and to love others.

How many of us suffer in our relationships, in our view of ourselves and our potential, because we have been presented with a distorted image?

- Maybe a parent made you feel unloved and unwanted.
- Maybe a teacher convinced you that you would never amount to anything.
- Perhaps a boss let you know how little he thought of you.
- Maybe you have been abused and sinned against, and you feel dirty and ashamed.
- Perhaps a spouse has chipped away at your self-belief, and you

feel like a failure.
- Perhaps the weight of your own mistakes and poor choices weighs on you daily.
- Maybe you became persuaded that if you were just a little prettier, a little smarter, a little less socially awkward, then you would be acceptable.

Over the years I have been a pastor, through hundreds of counseling appointments and pastoral conversations, I have seen the same issues surface again and again, with a common root cause: We look to the wrong places for our self-image.

Only when we understand how God sees us will we experience freedom. Understanding how we appear to God changes everything. Only when we appreciate to the depths of our being how precious and loved we are by our Creator and Savior can we truly move into the abundant life that he promised us.

In this book, I will examine different sources of our self-image and show you that you have a unique value to God, a special place in his plan. As the title says, "If God had a fridge, your picture would be on it!"

Don't leave yourself crippled emotionally, spiritually and psychologically. You deserve better and those who live and work with you certainly deserve better. Understand who you really are, shatter the shackles of toxic self-image and replace them with a view of yourself that will truly set you free to be all God intended you to be.

Don't wait any longer. Turn the page now, and start your discovery to a whole, new you.

For the rest of the book, please visit Amazon.com and search for "Glyn Norman"
You can choose Kindle or Paperback version.
For $2 off the regular price, purchase the paperback from here:
https://www.createspace.com/4089387
and enter the code: TM244MX

Made in the USA
Las Vegas, NV
28 February 2023